EARTHQUAKES AND VOLCANOES

Sara Steel

Adam & Charles
Black · London

Black's Junior Reference Books
General Editor R J Unstead

Steel, Sara
Earthquakes and volcanoes – (Junior reference : 36)
1. Earthquakes – Juvenile literature
I. Title
551.2'2   QE521.3

ISBN 0-7136-2239-3

Published by A&C Black (Publishers) Limited, 35 Bedford Row, London WC1R 4JH
First published 1982

Filmset by August Filmsetting, Warrington, Cheshire
Printed in Hong Kong by Dai Nippon Printing Co. Ltd

Contents

1 What causes earthquakes and volcanoes?

Martha Repetto lived on Tristan da Cunha, a lonely island in the South Atlantic Ocean, 3 200 kilometres from the Cape of Good Hope. On the 10th October, 1961, Martha was looking for sheep on the lower slopes of Tristan's extinct volcano. For the last few days there had been strange rumblings from deep inside the volcano and the ground had trembled. That afternoon, there was a roaring sound, louder than the thunder which crashed in violent storms around the island.

Suddenly, with a terrible cracking noise, the earth split open in front of Martha. She tried to run back to the cottages, but huge chasms blocked the path. Sheep bleated in panic as they disappeared into cracks in the ground. The cracks quickly closed up again, pushing out high ridges of rock and stone from inside the earth. A mound of earth and rock 20 metres high rose up behind her and enormous boulders began to roll down the volcano towards the cottages. As she ran, Martha stumbled over water-pipes which had been pushed out of the ground.

The islanders' cottages on Tristan da Cunha

William Reppetto, head man of the island

The islanders were gathered by their homes. Martha's father pointed to the volcano. Boiling hot lava was pouring down its slopes. In a few moments, the island's fish-canning factory was completely covered by the lava stream, even the 20 metre high radio mast. The lava flowed on, over the old jetty, spreading into the sea with a loud hissing noise and forming a new coastline.

A small fishing boat ferried the 264 islanders through the wild seas to a large rock. There, they spent the night. Eventually they were taken to England and stayed there for two years, while the volcano spat fire and lava.

They had left 15 gentle sheepdogs and all their livestock on Tristan da Cunha. When the first boats returned to Tristan, the islanders discovered that these dogs had killed the 700 sheep, all the calves and the penguins. The men shot the dogs and the women began to disinfect their homes, which were swarming with green blowflies attracted by the hundreds of dead sheep.

Luckily, although the lava had flowed for almost two years, it had stopped a few metres from the cottages. Only one thatched roof had been burnt by sparks from the volcano. The cows were caught and tamed, the cottages cleaned and the hens shooed outside once more.

Earthquakes and volcanoes often occur in the same places. If you look at the map below, you can see the 'danger spots' where volcanoes and earthquakes are most likely to occur. To understand why this happens, you have to know how earthquakes and volcanoes are caused.

The surface of the earth is called the *crust*. It is a layer of hard rock. Underneath this layer, the rock is so hot that it can flow like treacle. The crust floats on the softer rock below. But the crust is not all in one piece. It is broken up into *plates*, like giant pieces of a jigsaw puzzle. Because the plates are floating on the softer rock below, they can move nearer or further apart from each other. Sometimes, the edge

A map of the earth, showing how the crust is broken up into plates. Earthquakes and volcanoes often occur at plate edges

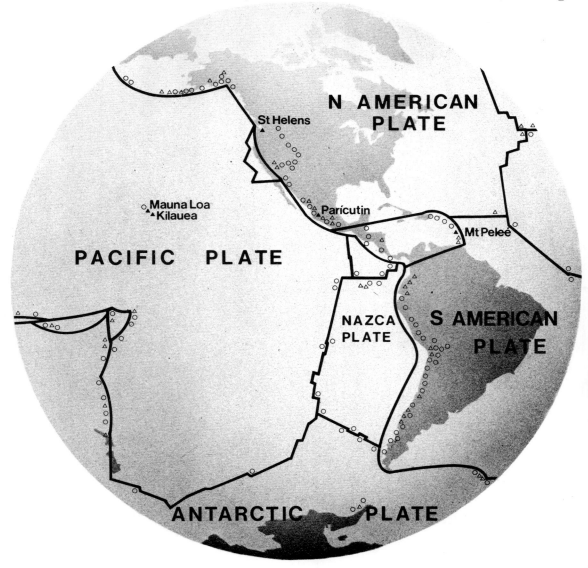

of one plate can grind against, or tear away from, the one next to it. This movement can cause earthquakes. Volcanic eruptions occur wherever the crust is weak, either thinner than usual, or cracked (faulted). As you can see on the map, volcanoes and earthquakes are most likely to occur around the edges of the plates.

Tristan da Cunha is at the southern edge of a great ridge which runs from north to south on the sea bed of the Atlantic Ocean. This ridge is where two pieces of the earth's crust are pulling away from each other. If you look at the map you can see that there are many earthquakes and volcanoes along the ridge.

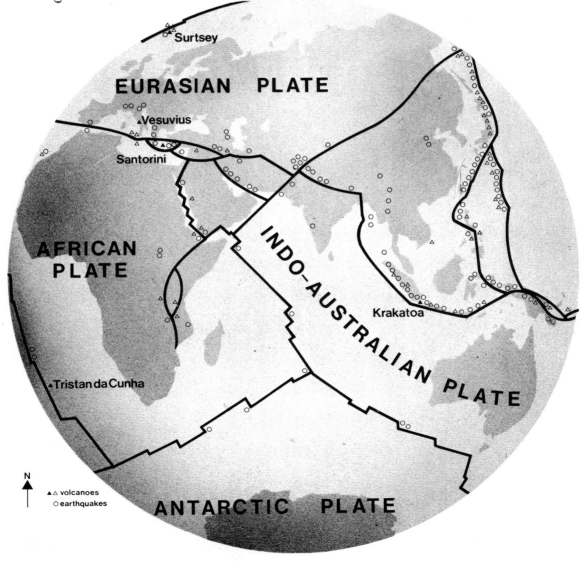

2 The trembling earth

A long time ago, people thought that earthquakes occurred when a god was angry. Port Royal, in Jamaica, was destroyed by an earthquake in 1692 and most people thought this was God's punishment for the wicked 'Pirate City'. In 1752, some very learned men of The Royal Society, in London, declared that 'Earthquakes only occur when people need chastening'.

Some people believed that earthquakes were caused by certain animals holding up the world. Indian children of North America were taught that a tortoise held the world on its back. When the tortoise moved, the earth trembled. Other stories tell of earthquakes caused by animals such as a hog scratching itself, or a whale twitching its tail. The legends of the Mayan people said that the gods held a cube-shaped earth and tipped it to shake off a few hundred people whenever there were too many!

The Ancient Greeks decided that earth tremors were the result of a god called Atlas trying to shift the weight of the world on his shoulders. A Greek

The ruins of City Hall, San Francisco, after the earthquake in 1906

philosopher, Aristotle, had a more scientific explanation. He said that rain had seeped into the earth, turned into a gas and was struggling to return to the air above.

Gradually, scientists realised that earthquakes were caused by some disturbance of the earth's crust. Now they know that when the plates grate against each other or tear apart, the rock is jarred and sends out shock waves. It is these shock waves which make the ground tremble and crack during an earthquake. You can feel shock waves through your own body when you jump awkwardly from a high place.

The first shock wave of an earthquake travels faster than a bullet, at 8 km a second. This is called the P wave (push wave). The second wave (S, or shake wave) shakes the ground like a dog shaking a rug.

As you are reading this, there will probably be an earthquake somewhere in the world. Every year, there are half a million earthquakes, though most of these can only be detected by special instruments, called *seismometers*, also called *seismographs*. The people of Japan have become used to frequent tremors – they have about 20 a day!

Most of the damage is done in under a minute, so it is not possible to run away from an earthquake. In the last 100 years, about a million people have been killed and 15 million injured in earthquakes,

During an earthquake, buildings usually collapse outwards and can block the streets. Rescue workers have to clear away the rubble before ambulances or cranes can be used

Wreckage left by the tsunami in
Japan, 1923

usually from the side effects of the tremors. Sometimes, people fall into the cracks which open up in
the ground, although this is unusual. However, in
the 1906 San Francisco earthquake, a farmer in
California was very upset when he saw his prize cow
disappear into a crack. When the gap closed up
again, only the cow's tail was left sticking out!

Deaths are usually caused by falling buildings,
explosions and fires from broken gas pipes or electric
cables, rivers bursting their banks, dams collapsing
or landslides. The most frightening cause of death is
probably the *tsunami*. These are huge waves which
can travel at speeds of 900 kilometres per hour.
Tsunami are sometimes called tidal waves, but they
have nothing to do with tides. They occur when an
earthquake or volcanic eruption disturbs the sea bed
and sends shock waves through the water. The wave
may be over 70 metres high when it reaches the shore.

Landslides often cause great damage after earthquakes. In 1920, there were so many earthquakes
and landslides in Kansu, Japan, that the people
could hardly recognise their own countryside. One
man had built a cabin on a hill. After a series of
tremors, he found that the cabin and the hill had
moved a kilometre from their previous position.

3 The earthquake's power

The place where an earthquake starts below the surface of the earth is called the *focus*. The point on the surface which is directly above the focus is called the *epicentre*.

The energy, or strength, of an earthquake is called its *magnitude*. It is measured by an instrument called a seismometer and given a number on a scale, called the Richter scale. Most strong earthquakes are between 3 and 8 magnitude. Each number on the Richter scale is ten times the last one, so a magnitude 8 earthquake is ten times the strength of a magnitude 7 earthquake. The strongest recorded earthquake was the one in Alaska (1964). It was 8.9 on the Richter Scale, the equivalent of 140 million tons of TNT explosive.

The shaking on the surface of the earth caused by an earthquake, is measured on the Mercalli Scale. This is estimated from eye witness reports and the amount of damage caused by the earthquake.

Deep cracks in the ground can be caused by an earthquake high on the Mercalli Scale

Roads were torn up and tram-lines broken during the San Francisco earthquake, 1906

Shock waves can cause brickwork to crumble

Poorly built buildings were reduced to rubble during the earthquake in Agadir, Morocco, 1960

The Mercalli Scale

I   Only seismographs can record this, though you may feel dizzy or sick. Birds and animals may be uneasy.

II   Hanging objects sway. Slight shaking at top of high buildings.

III   Felt by people. Parked cars rock gently.

IV   Doors, windows and dishes rattle.

V   Sleeping people wake, pictures fall, bells ring as towers sway, light furniture moves a little.

VI   Poorly built buildings are damaged and furniture overturned.

VII   Difficult to stand upright. Cars go out of control, most ordinary buildings damaged.

VIII   Chimneys fall, people panic. Trees shake or break. Buildings collapse, even well-built buildings suffer damage.

IX   The ground opens, underground pipes break.

X   Wide chasms appear in the ground. All buildings damaged.

XI   Stone buildings destroyed, railway lines twisted.

XII   All man-made structures damaged. The surface of the earth is changed.

4 The strongest earthquake ever known

Lisbon, Portugal: 1st November, 1755

All Europe felt the tremor that shook and destroyed the city of Lisbon. Chandeliers swung wildly in thousands of churches, where people were celebrating All Saints' Day. The water in Norwegian lakes and Scottish lochs became agitated and, in Holland, the steel cables of ships were snapped by the violent jolt. In Scotland, a preacher was amazed to see his congregation lurch from side to side.

The earthquake lasted for six minutes. Although it was never measured, it is believed to have been from 8.75 to 9 on the Richter Scale, the strongest earthquake ever known.

In the autumn of 1755, Robin Clarke celebrated his fourteenth birthday by sailing to the city of Lisbon with his father. The huge city was built on hills and the streets were narrow and steep. Most of the houses were built of stone and some were up to four storeys high. Lisbon was full of people from the surrounding villages and towns, preparing to celebrate All Saints' Day. Robin and his father spent a week exploring the city, then set sail just before dawn on 1st November.

The city of Lisbon before the earthquake in 1775

An artist's impression of Lisbon harbour during the earthquake

When the ship reached the centre of the harbour, it lurched suddenly as if it had run aground, although it was in deep water. Captain Clarke saw a tower falling in the city, then the buildings swayed backwards and forwards like a field of corn in the wind. He knew immediately that this was an earthquake. It was not possible to help the people in Lisbon. He had to sail for the open sea, or his ship would have been caught in the tsunami which was bound to come.

In Lisbon, there was a thunderous roaring as the earth trembled and buildings collapsed, weakened by continual shaking. The city was full of dust clouds which darkened the sky. The ground swayed from side to side, then up and down. Thousands of people rushed to the quayside to escape in boats. There was another great tremor and the huge stone quay collapsed into the sea, drowning hundreds of people.

The overturned candles in the churches and the cooking fires in the wooden houses caused fires to rage through the city. People were trapped in the flames and priceless papers, books and paintings were destroyed.

After more tremors, the bay drained dry. Everyone ran to look at the amazing sight of the sea bed and the stranded sea creatures. Suddenly, there was a deafening roar and a wall of water appeared like a black hill, hurtling towards Lisbon faster than an express train. The damage was terrible; 32 churches and 53 palace buildings were destroyed and only 3 000 of the 20 000 houses were left standing. Thousands of bodies were buried in the rubble and hundreds of people had been swept into the Atlantic Ocean by the tsunami. The great wave swelled to a height of 15 metres and travelled hundreds of kilometres to the coast of Morocco, where it swept ten thousand people to their death. In the West Indies, 5 500 kilometres away, the tides rose up to six metres and the water was a filthy black colour.

The bodies in Lisbon were a great problem to the rescuers. They were rotting in the warm autumn weather and there was a danger of disease. After a great deal of argument, the corpses were loaded on to old boats and sunk far out at sea.

When Lisbon was rebuilt, the houses were made stronger and the streets widened, so that if there was another earthquake, falling buildings would not block the streets. It took many years before the city was restored to its former beauty.

The ruins of Lisbon after the earthquake

5 A deep earthquake

Assam Province, India : 12th June, 1897

The Assam earthquake had its focus deep down in the earth's crust, and caused terrible damage over a vast area. In 15 seconds, 389 376 square kilometres was in ruins, all communications broken, hills torn apart and plains scarred by deep cracks, out of which spurted sand and water. Some of the fountains of sand were discoloured by coal, peat, resin, petrified wood or by a black earth quite unknown in the area.

The first tremor was followed by several aftershocks. It was impossible to stand up as the ground jerked backwards and forwards, then wobbled like jelly, making people feel seasick. In places, the waves in the ground were a metre high.

All stone buildings were flattened into heaps of loose stones, topped by whatever remained of the roofs. The thundering noise of the earthquake was so great, that even falling buildings went unheard. Villages and houses sank into the ground and disappeared.

Credgwell Lodge, in Assam, before the earthquake

The tremors continued all through that night, until several hundred had been counted. Over the next month they slowly decreased to about ten a day.

When government agents were able to ride into Assam and inspect the damage, they heard extraordinary tales. A river bed had risen six metres and dropped down again, wells had filled with sand or overflowed with stinking water. One man reported that his two elephants, his horses and dogs had all been knocked to the ground by the shock! Hills had moved backwards and forwards, lighthouses had swayed and steel railway lines were crumpled into twisted wreckage. One river had changed direction. Rivers had dried up and provided plenty of stranded fish for local people. The deep Singra river became so shallow that flat canoes were grounded.

The whole plain of Assam had been raised and the landscape changed. The earthquake was felt in Rome, Strassburg and Edinburgh. It was one of the deepest and most widely felt earthquakes.

Credgwell Lodge after the earthquake

6 The San Francisco earthquake

San Francisco, USA: 18th April, 1906

During the mid 19th century, thousands of American people left their homes and went to California to look for gold. Many of them settled in San Francisco. This tiny village grew into a city of nearly 50 000 people. No one knew that the city lay right across a crack, or fault, in the earth's crust, now called the San Andreas Fault.

The rocks on either side of a fault are under great strain. Sometimes the pressure becomes so great that the rocks slip past each other with a rush and create shock waves. In the 1906 earthquake, the rock moved seven metres northwards and caused terrible damage.

On the day of the earthquake, the people of San Francisco were celebrating the arrival of the famous Italian opera singer, Enrico Caruso. During the week before, Vesuvius in Italy, had erupted and the people of San Francisco had sent a large sum of money to the survivors. Caruso was looking forward to singing for these generous people.

Hill Street, San Francisco, after the earthquake

At 5.00 in the morning there was a deep rumbling noise and the brick streets of San Francisco rippled like a snaking rope. Electric cables broke and flashed blue sparks; water sprayed into the air from broken pipes and there was a smell of gas everywhere. Those who rushed outside were crushed to death as buildings collapsed with deafening roars and clouds of dust.

Caruso ran out onto the balcony of his hotel, terrified that his voice had been damaged by the shock. He amazed the panic-stricken crowds below by singing at the top of his voice! But he never sang in San Francisco again; he escaped and refused to return.

A strong wind blew up, fanning the flames from fires caused by broken cables and open cooking stoves. One woman cooked breakfast, without realising that the chimney of her stove had collapsed. The chimney caught fire and the flames spread rapidly, burning down a large section of the city. This was called the 'Ham and Eggs' fire.

When firemen tried to put the fires out, they were horrified to discover that the water supply was only a slow trickle, which eventually stopped altogether. The mains water pipes had been laid right across the fault line and were broken. The firemen used

Supplies soon became short and people had to queue for food. Soldiers patrolled the streets to prevent looting

Helpers set up an open air canteen in the street

The 'Ham and Eggs Fire'

After the fire, only the brick chimneys were left standing on Nob Hill, San Francisco. There have been 15 major earthquakes in California since 1906

every liquid they could find, including barrels of vinegar and crates of wine and beer. Parts of the city were blown up in an attempt to save the rest, but without success. The people had to watch their city burn. The fire raged for three days until the rains came, welcomed by great cheers from the survivors. But by that time, most of San Francisco had been destroyed.

There was no water, light or heat for the refugees. Soon, gangs of looters were stealing food and robbing people. A jeweller's wife managed to hide some of her jewellery. She covered her hands and wrists in jewels, and her husband bandaged her hands to hide the jewels!

After a while, food and hospital boats arrived and fifty thousand homeless people were shipped across the bay to a camp. Over 300 000 were given free travel by the railway companies, to escape from the ruined city.

It is believed there will be another major earthquake in California within the next ten years, perhaps stronger than the 8.2 earthquake in 1906. A great deal of money is spent preparing rescue services for such a disaster, but these squads hope that their services will never be needed.

7 The most destructive earthquake

Tokyo in ruins, 1923

Tokyo, Japan: 1st September, 1923

At two minutes to noon, the great clock in Tokyo stopped. Tokyo Bay shook as if a huge rug had been pulled from under it. Towering above the bay, the 4 000 metre Mount Fujiyama stood above a deep trench in the sea. It was from this trench that the earthquake came, at a magnitude of 8.3 on the Richter Scale.

The sea drew back for a few moments. Then, a huge wave swept over the city. Boats were carried inland and buildings and people were dragged out to sea. The tremors dislodged part of a hillside, which gave way, brushing trains, stations and bodies into the water below. Large sections of the sea bed sank 400 metres; the land rose by 250 metres in some places and sank in others. Three massive shocks wrecked the cities of Tokyo and Yokohama and, during the next six hours, there were 171 aftershocks.

At the Grand Hotel, Tokyo, the tall Mrs Morris Chichester-Smith was having a bath. As the hotel collapsed, she and her bath gracefully descended to the street, leaving both her and the bathwater intact!

Like the San Francisco disaster, fires had been lit for cooking. In the fragile Japanese houses, the open fires spread flames everywhere.

In Yokohama harbour, oil storage tanks burst into flames, creating a wall of fire. The flames were fanned by strong winds which rushed in to fill the vacuum as the hot air rose into the sky. A deadly gas was left after the fire had burnt up the oxygen in the air. Thousands of people who had managed to survive the earthquake, tsunami and fire, died from the poisonous carbon monoxide gas.

Thirty-eight thousand exhausted people fled to a camp a short distance from the blazing city. A fiery cyclone whirled into the camp and all but 30 people were burned to death.

The famous Tokyo Zoo was surrounded by fire and the keepers fought desperately to save the animals. Soon they realised how dangerous the animals would be if they escaped. In great distress, they shot all the animals except a tiny elephant, who was given a home by some refugees.

Tokyo burned until there was nothing left to burn. Over 143 000 people had been killed, 575 000 houses destroyed and the cost of the damage estimated at a billion pounds. It was the most destructive earthquake in history.

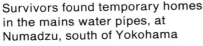

Survivors found temporary homes in the mains water pipes, at Numadzu, south of Yokohama

8 A shallow earthquake

Agadir, Morocco: 29th February, 1960

After the earthquake at Agadir, helpers had to clear away the rubble by hand

The temperature in the city of Agadir had soared to 40° Centigrade. Underneath the city, rocks were beginning to shudder and slip along a fault. For just 12 seconds the earth shivered, leapt sideways for over a metre and snapped back again. During this brief time, the mud and sheet-iron houses in the poor districts were destroyed. The foundations of the concrete buildings were so badly damaged that the buildings collapsed like a pack of cards. In that 12 seconds, 12 000 people died.

An earthquake which starts deep down in the earth's crust, like the Assam earthquake, causes damage for a great distance. A shallow earthquake, like the one at Agadir, causes terrible damage at the epicentre but is hardly noticeable a short distance away. After the Agadir earthquake, a plane from a nearby French aircraft carrier, 'La Fayette', flew over the scene. The pilot said the city looked as if a giant foot had stepped on it and squashed it flat. A kilometre away, there was no damage at all.

There were some extraordinarily lucky survivors in the ruined city. In the rubble of a hotel, French Marine rescuers heard the screams of a woman.

Victims were loaded onto stretchers and flown to hospital

23

During the night, they dug a shaft down through the rubble. They had to cut through each floor and move a few stones at a time. At last they found the trapped woman's feet. A doctor crawled down the shaft, felt the faint pulse in her ankle and said she was dying. Wearily, the Marines began to dig a second shaft, hoping they would be able to guess where her head was. It was over a day before they finally reached the woman again, and the searing heat made working in the dust and rubble nearly impossible. Eventually, the Marines managed to lift her out alive. She had been buried for nearly two days.

With the water supplies broken, there was a danger of disease from bodies rotting in the fierce heat, or of plague spreading. The survivors were hurriedly taken away from the city to refugee camps. Then, a terrible decision had to be taken. The conditions in the city were too dangerous for the rescuers. The people still trapped in the rubble would have to be abandoned.

The town was closed and strictly guarded. Men wearing protective clothing sprayed the whole town with disinfectant. Bulldozers rolled towards the city to crush the rubble flat, while a few gangs of brave men frantically searched with shovels and bare hands for anyone buried alive. A total of 21 people were taken out alive, before the town was finally smashed flat.

A car crushed under the rubble. It was estimated that 10 000 people were still trapped under the debris when the town was abandoned

9 The highest recorded tsunami

Alaska: 27th March, 1964

One of the earliest recorded earthquakes occurred on the first Good Friday, when Jesus was crucified. In the Bible, there is a description of the temple in Jerusalem being torn apart from top to bottom, as the earth shook and the ground opened up.

Another frightening earthquake occurred on a Good Friday in Alaska, nearly two thousand years later. It was the most violent tremor ever recorded, measuring 8.9 on the Richter Scale. If you look at the map on pages 6–7, you can see that Alaska is situated in a 'danger zone', where the Pacific plate slides under the American plate into a deep sea trench. The focus of the earthquake was 19 kilometres under the sea bed, just off the coast of Alaska.

If this earthquake had taken place in Europe, there would have been enormous loss of life and great damage, but fortunately the damage was restricted to mainly uninhabited areas. Even so, an astonishing £120 000 000 worth of damage was caused and the Alaskan town of Anchorage suffered disastrous damage. Its buildings collapsed without any warning and the ground rolled and rocked for four minutes. Great slabs of concrete smashed down into the street. One huge slab crushed a car with such force that the car was only knee high when the owner came to find it! Other cars bounced into the air as the ground flipped up and down. On one side of the main street, the ground beneath the shops dropped so that the shop roofs were at street level.

Houses and roads around Anchorage were destroyed as the earth shook. After the earthquake, unusually high waves were recorded as far away as South America

The earthquake caused some of the greatest changes to the surface of the earth ever recorded. There was devastation for 130 000 square kilometres and the earthquake was felt for over a million kilometres. Roads changed course, rose upwards and cracked across. Railway lines twisted into strange shapes. As the mountains shook, the rumbling of the earthquake was joined by the thundering of avalanches. Thousands of tonnes of snow and ice swept down, burying small cabins and villages. At the port of Seward, 320 kilometres from Anchorage, a landslide smashed oil-tanks which exploded, blasting flames across the town.

The earthquake rocked the sea bed, creating a tsunami 67 metres high, the highest ever recorded. Warnings were sent out around the world and prevented many deaths. The tsunami reached Hawaii in six hours and Japan in nine hours.

Although Alaska is remote, many harbours and fishing boats were destroyed by the tsunami. Craft of all sizes were sucked out to sea, never to be seen again. One fishing boat was lifted up and carried nearly two kilometres before it was set down on dry land, and another large ship was stranded on top of a school building!

The collapsed control tower at Anchorage International Airport

10 An earthquake destroys El Asnam

Rescue workers at El Asnam

El Asnam, Algeria: 10th October, 1980

Soldiers, firemen and shopkeepers worked alongside each other, grimly sorting through the rubble which was once a new city. Some of them remembered the last serious earthquake which had destroyed their city in 1954. The town had been rebuilt after that, but a terrible mistake had been made. The new town was built on a major fault line between two mountain ranges. The 1980 earthquake struck without warning and two massive tremors destroyed the new town. The first shock even broke the measuring instruments in Sweden, after registering 7.5 magnitude.

Huge rescue operations were started immediately. Emergency services travelled through the night and began to work under hastily erected flood-lights. Messages were flashed to international groups, such as the Red Cross, and requests for tents, blankets, water-purifying tablets, food and blood were sent to the world's disaster units. Jet planes flew in with tonnes of emergency supplies. France and Switzerland sent rescue teams with dogs, to look for survivors buried in the rubble. All off-duty nurses and

Deep cracks in the road, caused by the Algerian earthquake

Earthquakes can cause the foundations of buildings to subside

soldiers were told to report to their hospitals and barracks and to prepare for many days of working without rest.

Deep cracks (fissures) across the town had ruined roads and homes. In a modern hotel, 800 people had been eating lunch. After the tremor, the huge concrete roof lay at floor level; the people were crushed underneath. Over 1 000 people had been in the mosque; all were dead.

As they worked, rescuers constantly heard cries coming from beneath the rubble. Two days after the earthquake, a two month old baby was found, crying but unharmed.

It was estimated that 20 000 people had died, 50 000 were injured and 300 000 were homeless. After two weeks, some of the rescuers were exhausted and ready to give up. They were delighted when six people were found after being buried alive in a cafe. The survivors had lived mainly on the cafe's stocks of lemonade.

When the earthquake struck, farmer Mohamed Sabi and his family were strolling through the modern shopping centre in El Asnam. The ground rocked and rumbled under his feet and he suddenly found himself in darkness. The huge shopping centre had collapsed into a pile of rubble. Mohamed Sabi was in a small space just large enough for his body, but his legs were trapped and he could not move.

Outside, rescuers eventually decided that no-one could be alive under the tightly packed rubble. Bulldozers shovelled up the concrete. The drivers were very tired and went to have a coffee break. The first driver to return heard a groaning noise just in front of his bulldozer. The other drivers ran up and they carefully began to remove the rubble by hand. A doctor crawled in under a slab of concrete to reach Sabi. Just then, there was another tremor. Everyone held their breath but the concrete slab stayed firm and, eight hours later, Sabi was eased out. The doctor could not understand how Sabi had lived through such an experience. Mohamed Sabi was 74 years old!

Survivors at El Asnam made camp out in the open, in case there were more tremors

11 Disaster in southern Italy

Eboli, Nr. Naples, Italy: 23rd November, 1980

Just one month after the disaster at El Asnam, a sixty second earthquake rocked southern Italy and demolished 90 towns and villages. The focus of the earthquake was under the mountain town of Eboli. Unfortunately, rescue services were not as well organised as they had been in Algeria.

It was night time when the earthquake struck. Remote mountain villages were shaken and buildings slipped down the mountainside in great flurries of dust.

Soon fog, lashing rain and then snow hit the isolated mountain villages. The landslides had made the roads impassable and the villagers knew it would be days before rescue teams came to help them. Four days after the earthquake, reporters were able to reach the villages, but it was weeks before any help arrived. In a desperate radio call, the Mayor of Baragiano village cried, 'We are 3 000. We are cut off, cold and hungry. We have no food, blankets or tents. In the name of Almighty God, when are you going to come?'

San Lorenzo, one of the many mountain villages destroyed by the 1980 earthquake in Italy

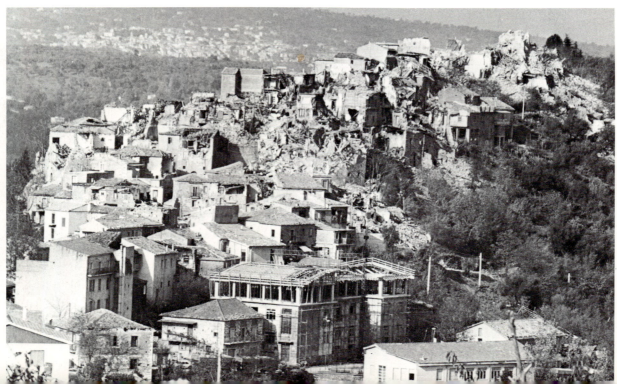

The freezing weather continued. Thousands of people were living out in the streets, or in cars. There was a sea of mud. All around, there was moaning, crying and knocking from people buried in the rubble. But there were too few helpers; each piece of rubble had to be moved by hand.

When rescuers finally arrived, the villages were disease-ridden. The ruins were sprayed with disinfectant and the rescuers had to wash themselves in disinfectant every day.

Two months after the earthquake, some people were still living in caravans, metal shelters, unheated tents or in ships in the Bay of Naples. It was one of the coldest winters Italy has ever known. There were many arguments about the design of buildings which had collapsed and the delay in organising relief for the survivors.

Yet there was one piece of good luck. A fireman was clearing rubble in the church of St. Theodore, when he discovered a chest full of gold coins under the floor. This was the treasure of St. Theodore. The treasure had been talked about for hundreds of years but, until the earthquake, no-one could find it.

Huge quantities of food and clothing were sent to Southern Italy after the earthquake. They were left to rot in the streets. Survivors needed tents and medical supplies instead

Trained dogs helped to find people buried in the rubble

12 The story of volcanoes

A legend told to Yana Indian children of North America tells how fire was captured from a volcano. It says that a man stole some of this fire and ran home with it. On his way home he stumbled and dropped the fire, which set the whole world alight.

There are many such stories and some of them are probably quite close to the truth. Erupting volcanoes may well have set the countryside on fire. It is possible that people would have saved burning branches to frighten away wild animals, give light during the dark winter days and make fires for cooking.

Like earthquakes, volcanoes were thought to be the sign of an angry god. A famous Roman poet, called Virgil, said that the Mount Etna volcano was the prison of a giant called Enceladus. Occasionally, Enceladus would wake up and struggle to free himself.

Vulcan pounding on his anvil

To the north of Sicily, there is a volcano called Vulcano. The Greeks called it 'The Chimney of the God of Fire' and the Romans named it after Vulcan, who was said to be the blacksmith to the gods. Vulcano was believed to be a forge, bellowing out smoke and fire, and the explosions were Vulcan pounding on his anvil.

Some Greek philosophers tried to find more scientific reasons for volcanic eruptions. Two thousand years ago, it was suggested that there were winds underground trying to escape. Shakespeare believed this theory and in his play 'Henry IV' he wrote that the earth was shaken 'by the imprisoning of unruly winds'.

People who study volcanoes nowadays are called vulcanologists. Their job is to find out how volcanoes are caused.

Pressures and movements in the earth's crust, especially at plate edges, cause rocks to grind against each other. This creates such intense heat that rock is melted. The molten rock can rise up to the surface through any crack, or fault, in the crust. If you look at the map on pages 6–7, you can see the volcanoes around the plate edges. The Pacific Ocean is nearly surrounded by volcanoes and this volcanic belt is called 'The Ring of Fire'.

'Pele's Hair', formed from wind-swept molten lava. At one time, Hawaiians believed that Pele was a fire goddess who lived in the crater at the top of Kilauea volcano, Hawaii

Stromboli volcano, Italy

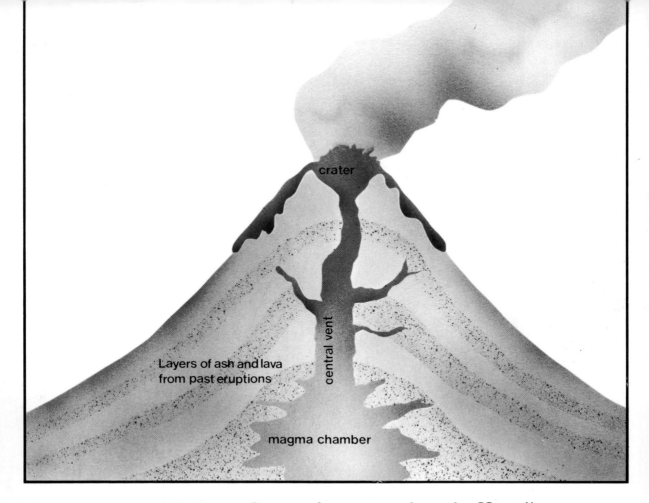

crater

central vent

Layers of ash and lava
from past eruptions

magma chamber

How a volcano is formed. Magma forces its way up the vent. The volcano is built up from layers of ash and lava. Magma that reaches the surface is called lava.

Some volcanoes, such as the Hawaiian ones, are nowhere near plate edges. They are in places known as 'hot spots', where the crust of the earth is very thin and molten rock, called magma, can easily force its way through. Sometimes the magma collects in a magma chamber inside a volcano. As more magma seeps in, the chamber gradually swells up like a balloon. Eventually, the pressure is so great that the volcano erupts. Crater Lake, in Oregon USA, was formed by rainwater which collected in the collapsed magma chamber of Mount Mazama. Often, the top or side of a volcano is blown off by the eruption, leaving a huge crater. The largest crater in the world is Mount Aso in Japan, 114 kilometres around the rim and 36 kilometres across.

Volcanic eruptions can be of different strengths, depending on the temperature and the type of rock under the volcano. They range from the almost gentle Hawaiian type, to the violent Plinean and Pelean types. You will be reading about these later. The volcano on the island of Stromboli, off the north coast of Sicily, has given its name to mild gas eruptions. Stromboli is called 'the lighthouse of the Mediterranean', because it is always smoking by day and glowing red at night. It has been erupting for 2 500 years!

There are about 500 active volcanoes at the moment. An active volcano is one which has erupted within recorded history. A dormant volcano is one which may not have erupted for a thousand years or so, but is still in a 'trouble spot'. Sometimes, an extinct (dead) volcano can erupt. After 6 000 years, Helgafell in Iceland erupted in 1973, showering black ash over the nearby town of Heimay.

A street in the town of Heimay, before and after Helgafell erupted

The throne room in the Minoan palace at Knossos, Crete

Map showing the area covered by ash after the eruption on Santorini

13 The lost world of Atlantis
Santorini (Thera): 1477 BC

A volcano may have been responsible for one of the most mysterious disappearances in history. Historians never understood how the rich and powerful Minoan people of Crete vanished in the 15th century BC. At that time, people in the rest of Europe were living in primitive villages. But, on the islands of Crete and nearby Santorini, there were large well-organised cities. Then one day, the people of Santorini ceased to exist. Crete was covered in poisonous ash and buildings were blasted by explosions.

It is now thought that the destruction of these civilisations gave rise to legends about Atlantis. This land was said to be a paradise on earth, whose people led a way of life which was the envy of the world. The Greek writer, Plato, told the story in 'Timaeus': 'But at a later time there occurred portentous earthquakes and floods and one grievous day and night befell them when the whole body . . . of warriors was swallowed up by the earth and the island of Atlantis in like manner was swallowed up by the sea and vanished.'

In 1859, miners on Crete were digging ash for cement to build the Suez Canal. They uncovered intricate buildings 30 metres below the ground. Later, excavations revealed that there had been a huge volcanic eruption on the island of Santorini nearly three and a half thousand years ago. It was the biggest bang in the history of the world. The island was blown to pieces and caused huge tsunami which destroyed much of Crete, including Akrotiri, a huge town of 30 000 people.

It is now thought that the eruption on Santorini could explain one of the miracles told in the Bible. In the story which tells how Moses led his people to the Promised Land, the Bible mentions pillars of fire at night and pillars of cloud by day. These may have been caused by the volcano erupting 720 kilometres away at Santorini. Moses and the Israelites stopped on high ground by 'The Sea of Reeds' – not the Red Sea, but Lake Menzaleh on the Mediterranean coast of Egypt. As the Egyptian troops approached, a huge wall of water roared towards them, leaving Moses and his followers safe on the hills.

This, it is suggested, was the tsunami caused by the volcanic explosion on Santorini. Archaeologists hope to excavate the area where the Egyptian soldiers drowned, to search for swords, chariots and the bones of horses and men.

An ornamental bull's head, found at Knossos

The palace of Phaestos, Crete. Built in about 1750 BC, it was hidden under volcanic ash for over a thousand years

A street in Pompeii

14 The hidden city of Pompeii

Pompeii, Italy: AD 79

One of the most famous volcanoes in the world is Vesuvius, near the town of Pompeii, in Italy. Vesuvius was peaceful and dormant for hundreds of years. Few people realised they were living on the slopes of a volcano. The soil was fertile and there were vineyards growing on the slopes of the mountain, right up to the mouth of the crater.

Earthquakes are often a warning that a volcano is likely to erupt and, in AD 62, there was a severe earthquake which damaged Pompeii. During the next 16 years there were many earthquakes. But the area was prosperous, so people just shrugged their shoulders and repaired the damage. No-one knew there was a link between earthquakes and eruptions.

Although Vesuvius erupted nearly 2 000 years ago, we have an eye witness account of the eruption. It was written by the nephew of the famous Roman writer, Pliny. Violent eruptions have been called Plinean ever since.

Pliny's nephew said that there was a sound like a thunderclap. An enormous cloud gathered in the sky over the volcano and began to rain huge pumice stones and ash. The terrified people held pillows over their heads for protection. Over threequarters of the mountain was blasted across the countryside. The cloud spread till it blocked out the sun, and the sky was dark for three days. Many people were killed by the poisonous sulphur gas. Some of the bodies, discovered later, had their hands over their mouths, as if they were desperately trying to keep out the fumes. Others were buried under collapsing buildings, burnt to death in fires started by the hot ash, or killed by rocks flung out of the volcano. Volcanic ash gradually built up against doors and windows and trapped people who had sheltered indoors. Many people did manage to escape, but 16 000 are thought to have died.

Pliny died of a heart attack; his nephew and the rest of the family joined the thousands of others trying to escape. They reached a hill and watched as the sea drew back, leaving fish stranded on the sea bed. Those on low ground were horrified to see a

The bodies of those killed at Pompeii had left hollows in the hardened ash. When plaster was poured into the hollows, the body shapes could be seen, just as they were when the people died

Herculaneum

wall of water rushing towards them, drowning hundreds of people who had hoped to escape by boat.

Torrential storms turned the volcanic ash and pumice into thick mud which swept down over the nearby town of Herculaneum. The town was buried in cemented mud, 22 metres deep.

Pompeii and Herculaneum were so well hidden by ash and mud, that after a while everyone forgot they were there! Their secrets stayed buried until the late 17th century. Then, parts of the buried towns were uncovered when an irrigation channel was dug. In 1860, archeologists began careful excavation of the towns.

They uncovered scenes of death and destruction. Some skeletons were found, but most of the bodies had decayed, leaving their shapes imprinted in the hardened ash.

Even food was found, laid out on tables and preserved by the ash cement. There were charred loaves of bread, nuts, figs and even eggs with their shells still intact.

One of the most famous discoveries at Pompeii was a watch dog, wearing a thick collar chained to a post. An imprint of the dog's body had been left in the hardened ash

15 Krakatoa, the explosion that rocked the world

Krakatoa, Indonesia: 26th August, 1883

In the late 19th century, there was a tremendous explosion on Krakatoa, a small island in the Sunda Strait between Java and Sumatra. The sound of the explosion travelled at 1 004 kilometres per hour, breaking windows and cracking walls for thousands of kilometres.

One and a half days after the eruption of Krakatoa, the blast of air reached London. The dust caused by the explosion collected high up in the atmosphere and blocked out some of the heat and light from the sun. The world was plunged into years of cool summers and freezing winters. In the South Seas, rain completely blotted out the sun for two days.

Brilliant sunsets were caused by the dust. First, the sun appeared to be green, then bright blue and for three years afterwards it had a pink ring around it. Vivid rainbows appeared as the sun set and, at night, even the stars and moon looked green.

The island of Krakatoa was in the busy sea lane between Java and Sumatra. No-one knew that it

Map showing the effects of the eruption of Krakatoa

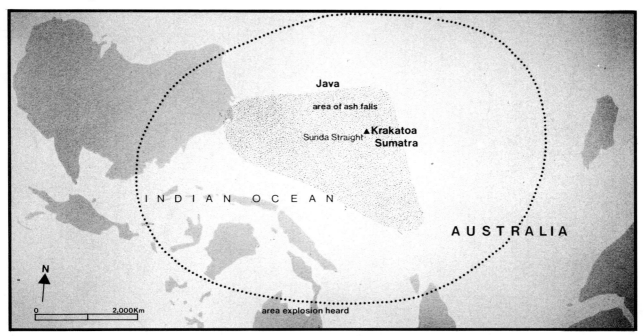

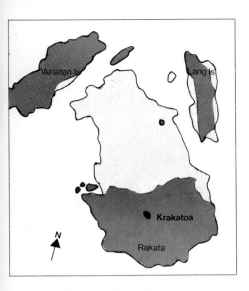

Map showing how the islands changed after the eruption of Krakatoa. The dark grey areas show what was left of Krakatoa and the surrounding islands after the eruption

lay directly above a gigantic crack in the earth's crust. Below, was a reservoir of white-hot magma. In the 1870's, earthquakes opened the crack and sea water seeped down into the magma chamber. The boiling water inside the chamber turned to steam. A mixture of explosive gases reacted with the magma to form pumice stone, which blocked any escape holes in the volcano. Pressure began to build up inside the chamber. Eventually, so much gas and magma was trapped inside the chamber that the pumice stone 'plugs' were blown out. At one pm on the 26th August, Krakatoa erupted.

Deafening explosions continued for five hours, even waking people in Australia. Five thousand kilometres away the explosions sounded like gunfire. Within an hour there was a column of cloud above Krakatoa, twice as high as Mount Everest.

For 18 months after the eruption, floating pumice blocked the shipping lanes. A vast area of sea around the island was dull grey and packed with the bodies of animals and fish.

On the final explosion, the sea and magma met once more. Almost the whole of the island was blown into the sky. Glowing, red-hot rocks lay 40 metres deep over an area of land larger than France.

Sailors in the area had to shovel ash off the decks of their ships as the vessels were in danger of sinking from the weight. Even more terrifying was the pink glow of phosphorescent light, called 'St. Elmo's Fire', which coated masts and rigging.

The greatest destruction was caused by the tsunami. After the final explosion, the sea retreated, then built up into a huge wall of black roaring water. The wave reached 35 metres high in some places and smashed everything in its path. A warship was pulled from its mooring and tossed far into the jungle. Lighthouses were swept away and 36 000 people were killed by the wave as it rushed along, carrying with it houses, rocks, trees and people. On nearby Sumatra, heavy treasure chests bolted to the ground, were picked up and swept along by the swirling waters.

An engraving from a photograph taken just after the eruption in 1883

After 11 hours, the tsunami reached Aden, 6 000 kilometres away. Two days after the explosion, the tsunami had travelled across the world, changing the level of water in the English Channel by five centimetres.

Surprisingly, some people on the nearby islands did survive. One man sat for hours on a dead cow and floated around until he was saved. Another man was carried along for half a kilometre and became wedged in a tree. He lost all his clothes but was unhurt!

Afterwards, the survivors had a terrible time. All the crops had been destroyed and fields were covered by lumps of coral from the sea, some as large as houses. Animals were either dead or starving. Worst of all, there was no water, all the rivers and lakes were covered in muddy ash.

In 1928, a small cone of rock pushed up in the sea beside the old crater. The people called it Anak Krakatoa, or 'child of Krakatoa'. The cone is believed to be directly over the huge fissure which caused the eruption in 1883. There was a further eruption in 1952 and everyone in the area wonders whether there will be another disaster.

Krakatoa erupts, 1883

16 The death cloud of Mount Pelée

Martinique, West Indies: 8th May, 1902

Auguste Ciparis was frightened. In his dark stone cell he was not sure of the time, but his stomach told him that he had not eaten for nearly a day. Some hours before, the walls of his cell had glowed red, turning the cramped space into a furnace. His body was terribly burnt and he could not stop trembling. He had shouted for hours, but the jailors would not come. Gradually, he became weaker and weaker.

Days later, the sound of voices woke him and he shouted as loudly as he could. When he was gently taken from his prison cell, he gasped in horror. The once busy, beautiful town of St. Pierre was smoking and silent, its buildings flattened. The smell of burning and gas was everywhere.

St. Pierre is a town on the island of Martinique, in the West Indies. Six kilometres from the town, is the island's volcano, Mount Pelée. In 1902, there were a few small eruptions which showered the town with light ash. In a letter to a friend, one lady

Headlines of 'The New York Times', May 11, 1902

Auguste Ciparis' stone cell

45

The nuée ardente rolling down the slopes of Mount Pelée

complained that the horses in the street were dying from the sulphur gas. The sounds in the street were muffled by the ash, but the town was thought to be safe and villagers hurried down from the volcano's slopes to stay in St. Pierre.

They watched as the sky above Mount Pelée glowed bright red, reflecting the pool of boiling lava welling up in the crater of the volcano. There was a tremor which stopped clocks, shifted tables, flung open doors and smashed china. A huge yellow cloud swirled into the sky. Then, the crater wall melted in the heat and burst open. Lava, rock and mud poured down in a searing flood, 40 metres high and half a kilometre wide. In its path lay a sugar factory. The deadly river completely covered the tall factory building, killing everyone inside, then flowed straight to the sea. The water boiled and drew back. Then, a huge wave thundered onto the town, causing panic as people trampled over each other trying to escape.

The vent of the volcano had become blocked with thick lava and enormous pressure built up as the gases seethed and boiled inside the volcano.

St. Pierre in ruins

The side of the volcano turned red and swelled up like a balloon. A series of deafening explosions followed and black clouds of ash darkened the sky.

In St. Pierre, the people watched in terror as the side of the mountain burst open. A huge glowing gas cloud, 400 metres high, rolled out, followed by a whirlwind of steam and ash. In two minutes, the cloud had rolled down the mountain and was over the town. All but two of the 30 000 people were killed and the whole town was completely ruined. Great stores of rum in the town caught fire. The flames spread across the island, but no-one was left alive to stop the blaze.

When the glowing gas cloud reached the sea, the water boiled and ships moored in the harbour were set alight by a rain of hot ashes.

The gas cloud was later called a 'nuée ardente' (glowing cloud). It had blown down walls a metre thick and shifted a three tonne statue across a square.

Auguste Ciparis was lucky, but he lived a strange life after recovering from his burns. He travelled with a circus, shut in a cell like the one on St. Pierre and was exhibited as 'The Man Who Escaped Hell!'

17 Paricutin, the birth of a volcano

Paricutin, Mexico: 20th February, 1943

It was a cold February day in the village of Paricutin, 320 kilometres west of Mexico City. The local people were gathered in the church, praying that the earthquakes would soon stop. During that day, there had been 300 small earthquakes.

The tremors had prevented a local farmer, Dionisio Pulido, from ploughing his field. On the 20th February the tremors stopped and Pulido hitched his oxen to the plough. The soil was warm under his bare feet, warmer than usual for February. He stopped in surprise. There had always been a small pit in his cornfield, but now it seemed larger and there was smoke rising from it. He heard a deep rumbling beneath his feet. Then, to his astonishment the pine trees at the end of the field began to sway. The ground in front of him cracked and swelled up to the height of a man. Pulido ran away in terror as dust, ash and hot stones shot from the cracks, and sparks set the trees on fire. The smell of sulphur clung to his nostrils and Pulido was convinced it was the work of the devil.

That night, everyone left the village. Huge fire bombs were being blasted into the air from Pulido's field. In the morning, a cone as tall as a house stood in the field. It was pouring out smoke, tonnes of rocks and lava. The lava flowed all week, covering

The church at Paricutin, partly covered by lava

Paricutin volcano, Mexico

the whole of the town except the top of the church.

Dionisio Pulido had seen the birth of a volcano in his field. Within a month, Paricutin, as the volcano was called, had grown to a height of over 300 metres.

For nine years, enormous rocks were hurled out of the volcano. The explosions could be heard in Mexico City. The countryside around Paricutin was so thickly covered with ash that the cattle grew thin, then died from lack of grazing. Water was scarce because the rivers were clogged with ash and rocks. Birds were overcome by poisonous gases and dropped dead from the sky.

In 1952, Paricutin stopped erupting. It was then 410 metres above the cornfield. Dionisio had lost some of his farming land, but lived to tell an amazing story to his grandchildren!

Paricutin was not the only volcano to rise from farming land in Mexico. In 1759, the Jorullo volcano was formed in the middle of a plain and destroyed fields of sugar cane. It erupted for 15 years. In 1770, the Izalco volcano rose up through a cattle ranch. This volcano is now 2 000 metres high, still growing, and highly active.

Mauna Loa erupts

18 Kilauea, the highest lava fountain

Hawaii: 14th November, 1959

The eruptions at Thera, Pompeii and Krakatoa are called Plinean. These are the most violent kind of volcanic eruption. They occur when the vent of a volcano is blocked. Gases and magma build up inside the volcano and finally explode in huge eruptions. The more 'gentle' type of eruption is called Hawaiian. These occur when the magma is liquid, fast flowing and can easily escape through the vent.

The Hawaiian Islands were formed from layer upon layer of lava, which spurted out from the sea bed. Generally, the volcanic eruptions on Hawaii are safe enough to be watched by thousands of tourists. Sometimes, people can even get to within a few metres of a lava flow.

The shield-shaped Mauna Loa volcano, in Hawaii, is probably the largest mountain in the world, and the largest active volcano. Its peak is 9 660 metres above the ocean floor. Mauna Loa has a rhythm of eruptions about every three and a half years. Over a billion tonnes of lava have poured down its slopes.

The nearby volcano, Kilauea, is equally famous. In 1790, a Hawaiian chief and his warriors were marching 10 kilometres from the Kilauea crater when there was a sudden eruption of hot mud and ash. The men were all killed, and their footprints can still be seen in the hardened clay.

In the crater at the top of Kilauea, there is a lake of red-hot lava. This fiery lake is called Halemaumau, or 'The Fire Pit'. The lake is formed from two million tonnes of liquid rock at a temperature of about 800 degrees Centigrade. Experts estimate that the lake will take over a century to cool.

On the 14th November, 1959, there were 2 000 tremors from deep down in Kilauea's crater. Vulcanologists from all over the world rushed to Hawaii, to wait for an eruption. Watching from the observatory on the slopes of the volcano, they were rewarded by the sight of the highest lava fountain ever recorded – over 600 metres of spurting red lava. The fountain played for hours, scorching the faces of the observers with its searing heat. One man wrote that the sulphur fumes gave everyone a sore throat and that watching the display was rather like standing behind a jet plane when its engines started.

The 'Fire Pit' in the crater of Kilauea

19 Surtsey Island

Surtsey, Iceland: 14th November, 1963

Like Hawaii, Iceland has been formed from lava, which flowed through cracks in the earth's crust. Iceland is at the northern end of the Mid-Atlantic Ridge, where two plates are pulling apart. There are many volcanoes in the area and over 30 have erupted in the last thousand years.

The eruption off the coast of Iceland in 1963 was one of the most exciting in recent years. The captain of a fishing boat sighted a column of smoke rising from the sea. Sailing closer, the crew could smell sulphur and noticed that the sea was glowing and very warm. The column of smoke rose from a ball of white steam on the surface of the sea. Whirlwinds circled the boat. Ash, cinders and enormous hailstones drummed on the deck.

A volcano had erupted on the sea bed and the magma had been cooled by the sea to form an island. This island was named Surtsey, after a giant Norse God called Surtur. That night, the island was 11 metres high. Four days later it was as high as two houses and 650 metres long.

Volcanic eruption from the sea bed, Surtsey, 1963. This picture was taken about three hours after the eruption started

Surtsey island being formed from volcanic lava

Sigurdur Thorarinsson, an Icelandic geologist, described the new island: 'When darkness fell it was a pillar of fire and the entire cone was aglow with bombs which rolled down the slopes into the white surf around the island. Flashes of lightning lit up the eruption cloud and peals of thunder cracked above our heads.'

Scientists from all over the world came to see Surtsey. The island had only just been formed, so it was a wonderful opportunity for scientists to find out how animal and plant life develops. For two years the volcano continued to pour out lava and its shape changed constantly. Tall black cliffs were repeatedly washed away by the pounding seas, but the island began to take shape and was declared a nature sanctuary.

Naturalists landing on the black lava beach and dodging the lava bombs, reported that flies and butterflies were on the island. By 1967, Surtsey was nearly 200 metres high and 20 kilometres long. There were 23 species of bird, 22 species of insect and a variety of plants on the island. The clothes and shoes of the scientists, the sea, wings and fins had brought life to Surtsey.

Lightning flashes through the volcanic dust clouds over Surtsey

53

Mount St. Helens and surrounding area before the eruption in May 1980

20 Mount St. Helens erupts

Washington State, USA: 18th May, 1980

In March 1980, seismometers all round Washington State, USA, recorded strong earth tremors. The tremors were found to be coming from under Mount St. Helens, a dormant volcano in the state of Washington. Scientists reached the area the next day. They knew the earthquakes were a sign that a volcanic eruption would soon occur. But they did not know when it would happen. The area around St. Helens was closed off and forest wardens patrolled the roads to keep any curious people away. Scientists measured the crater shape and mountain sides and found that they were changing shape, until the north face of Mount St. Helens was bulging out by 100 metres.

On the 18th May, a magnitude five earthquake dislodged the bulging rock, creating the greatest landslide ever recorded. There was a huge explosion and the top of the mountain was blown off. All day

and all night the mountain poured pumice, dust and ash. The geologists had estimated the force of the explosion by looking at past patterns of eruption. But they had made a mistake. An area far larger than they expected had been affected. Meltwater from the snow and flooding rivers combined with the landslides to create destructive floods.

Rescue services began to search the area but maps were useless: the countryside had changed too much. As far as 12 kilometres away from the volcano, the heat was so great that the rescuers had to wear protective clothing.

The eruption blasted over 2.7 cubic kilometres of ash into the air. The huge cloud of ash travelled at tremendous speed. One car travelling at 112 kilometres per hour was overtaken and buried by the ash cloud. Campers were blasted by a freezing wind which whirled ahead of the ash, then were nearly suffocated by the burning cinders. It was estimated that the ash was about 80 degrees Centigrade. A

Mount St. Helens and surrounding area after the eruption

Cold Water II Observatory Post, eight kilometres north-west of Mount St. Helens. The camp was destroyed during the eruption and a five tonne truck buried under volcanic ash

camera-man was caught in the eruption and continued to film as he stumbled in the darkness. The swirling ash made him cough violently, and he believed that each step would be his last. He wandered in the ash cloud for nine hours before being rescued.

A weather satellite took pictures to show the cloud moving across the United States. It was thought that thirty million tonnes of ash would stay in the atmosphere for a year or more. A cloud of dust and ash settled in the upper atmosphere, between 16 and 20 kilometres above the earth's surface, reducing the amount of sun which could reach the ground. Scientists predicted that it would change the weather.

All birds, mammals and fish in the blast area were killed and thousands of fir trees lay flattened by the force of the explosion. Yet, like Surtsey, it was not long before life was beginning again. There were even heat-loving fungi growing in large areas!

In the months following the eruption, thousands of tonnes of gas and steam flowed from the vent every day. Other eruptions occurred, but the seismologists were able to predict these. After the last eruption, in 1857, Mount St. Helens continued to erupt for the next 22 years!

21 Vulcanologists and seismologists

Vulcanologists, who study volcanoes, and seismologists, who study earthquakes, have two main aims. One is to discover more about the earth and its behaviour. The other is to predict eruptions and earthquakes, so lives can be saved.

For centuries, there have been attempts to measure and record earth tremors. In about AD 130 a Chinese astronomer called Chang Heng made the first seismograph to record earthquakes. It was a bronze jar covered by a copper dome, surrounded by eight dragons' heads, each holding a brass ball. A pendulum in the jar shook during an earthquake, causing a ball to fall out of a dragon's mouth and into the mouth of a brass frog. This showed the direction of the earthquake.

Later seismographs consisted of a weighted pen and a drum of paper. During a tremor, the drum would move under the pen, recording the amount of 'shake'. Other simple instruments included a teaspoon on a string, or a glass of water, to show the strength of the different shock waves. In the 1906 San Francisco earthquake, one seismologist worked out the strength of tremors by biting on his metal bedstead. The earth's vibrations were carried through the iron frame of his bed to the teeth and bones of his skull! Modern methods use magnetic tape or electric 'eyes'.

Seismogram (right) with seismograph (left). The seismogram measures the tremor. The seismograph records the magnitude of the tremor

Changes in the level of the ground are measured by tiltmeters. In the past, tiltmeters had water in them, which tipped when the level of the ground changed. Now they use laser beams which change length as mountain ranges or volcanoes shift.

After every earthquake or eruption, teams of experts survey, map, take aerial photographs, measure temperatures and depths and estimate the volume of rock falls. Satellites in space are equipped with infra-red cameras which record information about every disaster on the earth's surface. They also show the increase in rock or water temperature before an eruption. This information is very helpful as it is impossible to keep a watch on every volcano. Only the most dangerous volcanoes are watched all the time.

In China, there is an 'army' of 300 000 people who look out for any strange changes in the earth, or the level of water. Changes like these can often indicate an earthquake or eruption. In 1158, the River Thames, in London, dried up before an earthquake and wells filled with yellow or red water.

Vulcanologists at Mount Etna, Sicily

After the eruption of Helgafell, in 1973, vulcanologists tried to cool the lava by spraying it with water

Most seismologists and vulcanologists also watch the behaviour of animals. Many animals behave oddly before earthquakes or eruptions because they are sensitive to tiny vibrations in the earth. Rats and snakes creep from their holes, nocturnal animals come out in daylight and pheasants scream nervously. Before an earthquake in Guatemala (1976), goldfish jumped out of the water and landed on the floor!

Although it might be possible to save lives, it is often impossible to stop the destruction to property and the countryside. Some attempts have been made but none were very successful. When Manua Loa erupted, bombs were exploded to make a barrier against the liquid lava and hoses were turned on the lava to cool it. In 1669, at Catania near Etna, the people tried to stop a lava flow from ruining their city. Men covered themselves in wet cow skins for protection and pushed iron bars into the lava. This made the hotter lava, under the crusted top, spurt out in another direction. Unfortunately, the lava flowed towards another town. The furious inhabitants of this town turned the flow back to Catania and the whole city was destroyed.

22 People in earthquake and volcano zones

If volcanoes and earthquakes are so dangerous, why does anyone live near them? Thousands of people live in the San Francisco area, USA. They know that an earthquake may one day destroy their homes and perhaps even kill them, yet many of them behave as if it will never happen. The ancient city of Antioch, in Turkey, was rebuilt nine times after major earthquakes. Concepcion, in Chile, and Messina, in Sicily, were both destroyed five times. Etna has erupted eight times this century, yet a new housing estate has been built on 70 year old lava flows. One day, Etna may erupt as violently as it did in 1669, when 20 000 people were killed.

People stay in these dangerous places for a number of reasons. The land is usually very fertile in a volcanic area and excellent crops can be grown. Often, people refuse to abandon their homes in case they never return. An 84 year old man, Harry Truman, would not leave his home on Mount St. Helens and a television interview showed him defying the volcano's power. His house was covered by melted snow and mud; Harry Truman was never seen again.

Homeless after an earthquake in Guatemala, South America

A block of flats collapses during the Algerian earthquake in 1980

It would be impossible for the governments of the world to force people to live elsewhere, so they try to make buildings in these areas as safe as possible, or at least make sure that they will not collapse and block narrow streets.

When the ground shakes, it is important that a building either follows the shake or absorbs it. It is the vibration which causes buildings to collapse. Centuries ago, Inca buildings in South America were built of stone without mortar. Japanese houses were built on large stones in the earth and made of a light framework. Both these kinds of buildings could move without collapsing.

Nowadays, there are usually special building laws in earthquake zones. Buildings should be placed on solid rock, made of strong flexible steel and the fewer doors and windows the better. Some roofs have rubber pads, rather than tiles. Nuclear plants must be built to withstand major earthquake damage, and dams and bridges should be reinforced. The roof frames of Japanese houses often have extra supports and some houses are built with interlocking bricks, rather like the irregular stones used by the Incas. Soviet scientists plan to hang buildings from steel cables. They are building a 14 storey sky-scraper which will be suspended from reinforced concrete towers, able to withstand any tremor.

When Mount Etna erupted in 1947, villagers living on the slopes of the volcano prayed that their homes would be saved. Miraculously, the eruption subsided shortly afterwards

During the Italian earthquake in 1980, many people refused to leave their ruined homes

Villagers in Guatemala after their homes were destroyed by an earthquake in 1973

It is estimated that one million people have been killed in the last 100 years and 15 million injured in earthquakes. Only 210 000 have been killed by volcanic eruptions in 260 years. In 1556, in Shensi Province, China, it was estimated that 830 000 people died in one earthquake.

There has been some success in predicting earthquakes. In 1975, careful measurement by seismic stations and thousands of local people in the Liaoning province of North East China, showed unusual movements of the earth. It was almost certain there would be an earthquake. The huge Hai Chen city was immediately evacuated. Five hours later, when the earthquake struck, ninety percent of the city was destroyed. Thousands of lives had been saved. However, the next year an earthquake in Tangshan, China, resulted in 750 000 deaths; the greatest natural catastrophe in modern time. Out of 31 predictions in a two year period, 18 were correct, seven were doubtful and six were wrong. It will be a long time before people are safe from the destruction caused by earthquakes and volcanoes.

Some famous volcanoes

Lassen Peak, USA

Antofalla, Argentina, South America (6 440m).
Highest active volcano.

Coseguina, Nicaragua. In 1835, a huge eruption blew away the
summit. The blast was heard over a 500 km radius. Soldiers
reported for duty, thinking there was a war.

Cotopaxi, Ecuador, South America (6 200 m). In 1929, a 200
tonne boulder was hurled 14 km.

Fujiyama, Honshu, Japan (3 776 m). The Never Dying
Mountain. Fujiyama is a holy place – the highest mountain
in Japan and the most beautiful – snow covered, a perfect cone
formed of layers of ash and lava.

Hekla, Iceland (1 491 m). The Black Gate of Hell. It once
erupted for six years without stopping.

Katmai, Alaska. It erupted in 1912, so violently that dust fell for
three days and there was no daylight. The temperature fell by
one degree Centigrade and caused the Arctic ice to move south,
blocking shipping lanes.

Kilimanjaro, Kenya (5 895 m). There are 3 huge craters, now a
game reserve. The summit is always covered in snow, despite
being close to the equator.

Mayon, Luzon Isle, Philippines (2 421 m). This is thought to be
the most perfectly shaped cone. It erupts with violent
explosions and nuée ardentes.

Popocatapetl, Mexico, South America (5 452 m). Called the
Smoking Mountain. A legend tells of a prince and princess who
loved each other. When she died, he built two great pyramids
(two mountains), buried her body on one and lit a torch on the
other. There is a mountain close to Popocatapetl called
Ixtaccihuatl, or white woman.

Tambora, Sumbawa, Indonesia (2 851 m). In 1851 a tremendous
eruption ejected more material than any volcano in history –
including Santorini and Krakatoa. It lost 150 cubic kilometres
of rock. 10 000 died in the eruption, 80 000 died of hunger
because of the dust-covered land. This was the year Europe had
no summer.

Tarawera, New Zealand. The best known volcano on the north
island of New Zealand. It erupted violently in 1886, but luckily
few lives were lost.

Acknowledgments

Keystone Press Agency 1, 3, 9, 11a,
12, 23a, 23, 24, 29, 30, 31, 31a, 35, 50,
51. Hulton Picture Library 2, 4, 5, 8,
10, 11, 13, 15, 16, 17, 19, 19a, 20, 21,
33, 36, 38, 39, 42, 63. Barnabys
Picture Library 12a, 18. Mansell
Collection 14, 20a, 22, 32, 37a, 37,
39a, 40, 44. Frank Lane Agency 25,
26, 52, 52a, 53. Oxfam Visual Aids
Department 27, 28, 28a, 60, 60a, 62.
Geoscience Features 33a, 45, 46, 47,
48, 49, 56, 57, 58. Frost Historical
Newspaper Collection 45a.
Associated Press Agency 54, 55.
Tony Garrett 6, 7, 34, 36a, 41. Merlijn
Poort 16a, 18a, 21a, 43.

Index

More books to read

Earthquakes, W. Hirst (Basil Blackwell)

Earthquakes, Volcanoes and Mountains, Roger Clare (Macdonalds)

Volcanoes, Rupert Furneaux (Kestrel Books)

Volcanoes, Werner Kirst (Hart-Davis)

Hill of Fire, Thomas Phewis (Worlds Work)

Focus on Earth, Angela and Derek Lucas (Methuen)

Earthquakes and Volcanoes, Imeld and Robert Updegraff (Methuen)